sdrawckaB

Jennifer White

Presentation by *BookLeaf Publishing*

Web: www.bookleafpub.com

E-mail: info@bookleafpub.com

ISBN: 9789357740098

First edition 2023

ACKNOWLEDGEMENT

I want to thank my mom, for helping me perfect each poem.
I also want to thank my dad, for being a source of inspiration.

Dancing to Life's Rhythm

The beat, da-dum, the beat, da-dum,
The pulse of the beat,
I feel it, da-dum,
My heart leaps
Overjoyed,
Da-dum,
Suddenly,
It is gone,
I've lost the rhythm,
I've lost the beat,
My heart sinks...
Empty.

Now read it backwards.

Just Run

Do you ever want to just run?
Do you ever want to be completely done?
Do you want to take a deep breath,
To stop all that distress?
To stop and wonder why one's life is such a
mess?
To get away from those who think they care?
Just wish to say to them what you wouldn't dare?

How to accomplish a single life dream?
That which could easily make one simply beam
To see that it all gathers at the seam
Oh one great, gleeful team

But to scream and bellow
And see that life's not so yellow
Not so like the sun
Not so like the rainbows
More so like the rain
More so like the hail
The splinters and smashers
The cacklers and bashers
One's sweetest dreams tattered to ashes.

Now read it backwards.

Fits

Would that make us failures?
Hmmmm

If we could fits
If we would fits
If we should fits

But then

If we should stands outs
If we wanted to stands outs
If we could stands outs

Would that make us champions?

Hmmmm

Are we champions if we fit in?
Do somethings differents.
Should we stands outs?

Now read it backwards.

Go For It

Throw it
Chuck it
Hate it

Or take it
Wake it
Rate it

Go from there
Push
Go forward

Get it out
Let it out
Then
Take it

Use it
Free it
Go for it

Now read it backwards.

See

We go a way
We go another way.
Ferried here and there.
Carted around.

Do we ever get the choice?
Do we ever get the choice?
We are called the package
We are called the package, always.

Maybe we want to be the cart.
Maybe we want to be the driver
But not this time,
We are called the package.

Do we ever get the choice?
We are called the package
We are called the package, always.

We look down at the real ground
We look up into the blissful sky
To the dream
We feel a connection.
The dream never dies.

We are suddenly not the package
We are suddenly not ferried here and there
We are not carted around

Sometimes you just need to look up
Imagine what you could have
Sometimes you just need to see your own way.
Afterall, seeing is believing... But nobody ever
told you exactly how to see.

We are the cart
We are the ferriers
We are the transport
We are carving our road.

Now read it backwards.

Fear

To say hello.
To converse,
To not be so mellow,
To not have to rehearse

I don't want to be shy
Don't want to cry,
Don't want to die,
I don't want to belie

To have rid of this fear.
To talk and to laugh,
To be able to say dear,
To be lost of this faff

I don't want to be shy
Don't want to cry,
Don't want to die,
I don't want to belie

To let go of this terror
It would be the deepest pleasure

Now read backwards.

In the Light

In the light
I think I am honest...
I think I am loyal
I think you are master
I think you are everything.

In the shadows.
I think I am brutal...
I think I am confused
I think you are dirt
I think you are nothing

In the Sun
I think I am powerful...
I think I am regal
I think you are love
I think you are pleased

In the Dark
I think I am merciless...
I think I am scarred
I think you are hateful
I think you are disgust.

What you see depends on what I think of you
Because glass has a fine edge
Sometimes my reflection catches the flip side

Now read it backwards.

Listen

Can you not hear me?
I was talking
I was shouting
I was screaming

There you sit
Staring... Into the fire
You sit in your chair

Can you not see me?
I was waving me arms
I was rocking your shoulders
I was stomping my feet

There you sit
Staring... Into the fire
You sit in your chair

I stopped talking
I stopped waving
I stopped moving
I stopped feeling

You turn
You look at me

Now read it backwards.

They Say

They say
Time fixes everything
Time can't fix me

If you were broken for 100 years
You will not fix yourself
Yet time passes

I am broken
Time can't fix me

They say
Time is the greatest healer
Time can't heal me

If you fall ill and do not seek help
You will not heal by yourself
Yet time passes

I am ill
Time can't heal me

Time fixes everything
They say

Now read it backwards.

I Now Am Reborn

Wished I was different
Ashamed of who I was
So I sought to alter myself

Now I change my state
Alright...
Forget the eating
Forget the past

It is time to be reborn

Now I will become reprogrammed
Of all the chances I had
Wait for the risk I am going to take

Amid the chaos of my life
Measure my progress

Reaching high
Enjoying my goal
Bobbing and weaving
Over and over I somersault
Running toward the finish
Now I am there

Now read it backwards.

Freedom

Why try to fly
If all you do is fall
You don't want to fail
You just want to be free.

Why try to swim
If all you do is sink
You don't want to stop
You just want to succeed.

Why try to flap
If all you do is fall
You don't want to flop
You just want to feel free.

Why try to sail
If all you do is sink
You don't want to stick
You just want to be a success.

Now read it backwards.

Disy

Twittering, twittering
You gave me the letter
Like a beautiful bird
Tweet, tweet

Hesitating, hesitating
You wondered whether to follow
Like a cautious cat
Hesitant, hesitant

Stuttering, stuttering
You snuck inside my head
Like a spiteful stoat
Stutter, stutter

Stumbling, stumbling
You slip along my path
Like a sly salamander
Stumble, stumble

Falling, falling
You tried to reach me
Like a fumbling fish
Fall, fall

Don't look down.
I dragged you here
Selfishly.
You cannot save me.

Now read it backwards.

Desperate Darkness

Crushing darkness
There's no way out
Of course,
Dwindling dreams.

Desperate darkness
Hear my wish
To see the night sky
To breathe the night air

A torch burns
A torch flares
My path is lit

Desperate darkness
You heard my wish
To see the night sky
To breathe the night air

Wonder! Wonder!

Now read it backwards.

Together

You and I
We'll sail across the sky
On our little moonlit ride

Join me now
Until the end
Stick by my side

No,
You don't stay with me.
The gap between us grows wide
I say farewell
To my world and
Out goes the tide

Now read it backwards.

Sleep Tight

I was warned of terrible sleep,
You fall,
You burn,
You scream and you cry.

Yet there is another kind:

I was told of beautiful sleep
With sweet dreams
You fly,
You swim,
You shout and you play.

I love that sleep...
With the dancing dreams

Now read it backwards.

Goodbye

Forever
Goodbye, but not
For we shall meet again
Somewhere along a different road

"I'm not ready for you to go.
I need you here.
You can't leave me.
I need more time."

Speak fast
For my time has run near
I must go
Though I want to stay here

Now read it backwards.

Remember

I love you
I need you to know
You can't remember me but
I will never go

I love you
I will stay here
You will be cared for
My dear

I love you
I remember the good times
I remember the fun times
Even though you can't.

I love you
I'm here for you and
This is true.

Now read it backwards.

Flicker

Tears trickle tracks down my face
Warm, misty breath escapes
I am cold and empty
Blood-shot, swollen eyes stare solemnly
Hatred boils
It is the same every night
When I see
The Mirror

I am an empty, burnt out husk

Suddenly, a flicker...

The flicker of light
The flicker of hope
The flicker of love

Is that it there?
In the back of my mind?
In the dark corner of The Mirror
Straight, staring at me?
Through the glass?
Begging me to follow
Begging me to follow the flicker
Does it lead me where I want to go?

Where do I want to go?

The flicker fumes frighteningly
And glides glittering away
I reach.

The flicker of light
The flicker of hope
The flicker of love
It is all around.
I am encompassed.

It says that I have endured such tragedies and
that I will endure more hardships
Yet I am here,
I have survived so many
So why relent now?

It says "I am that flicker inside   you...
        That flicker of fire.
        I am the flicker of light
        I am the flicker of hope
        I am the flicker of love
        And therefore, I know   you
have all three
        So you are worthy to me"